Contents

Section 1:
Getting Started with ITIL 4

Welcome & What You'll Learn

Welcome to the exciting world of ITIL 4 and effective service management! This book, "The ITIL 4 Guide: Service Management Essentials," is your roadmap to understanding and applying the core concepts that shape successful service delivery in today's technology-driven landscape.

What is ITIL?

Let's begin by demystifying ITIL. The Information Technology Infrastructure Library (ITIL) is a globally recognized best practices framework used by organizations worldwide to streamline their IT operations and align IT services with business goals. ITIL isn't a rigid set of rules but a flexible collection of principles, processes, and tools that can be adapted to fit the specific needs of any organization, large or small.

The Evolution to ITIL 4

ITIL has been continually evolving to keep pace with the changing technology landscape. The latest iteration, ITIL 4, places a greater emphasis on:

- **Value Co-Creation:** It recognizes that the customer is an integral part of creating value, not just a recipient of services.

- **Agility and Adaptability:** ITIL 4 supports organizations in responding swiftly to evolving market conditions and customer needs.
- **Holistic Approach:** It stresses the importance of looking at the big picture for service delivery, involving all aspects of an organization.
- **Practical Guidance:** ITIL 4 is packed with actionable insights to help organizations improve efficiency and reduce costs through better service management.

What You'll Learn in This Book

This book is your comprehensive guide to mastering the ITIL 4 framework. Here's a taste of what you'll learn:

- **The Building Blocks of Service Management:** Understand the fundamental definitions of services, value, outcomes, costs, risks, utility, and warranty.
- **The Four Dimensions of Service Management:** Learn how Organizations and People, Information and Technology, Partners and Suppliers, and Value Streams and Processes work together for effective service delivery.
- **The Service Value System (SVS):** Explore the core components of ITIL 4 and how they interact to create value.
- **The Guiding Principles:** Understand the universal principles that guide decision-making in IT service management.
- **The Service Value Chain:** Get a deep understanding of the activities that transform inputs into valuable outputs.
- **ITIL Practices:** Discover the 34 ITIL practices that cover various aspects of service management, including incident management, problem management, change enablement, and more.
- **Applying ITIL in Your Organization:** Learn how to integrate and adapt ITIL concepts to improve your organization's IT service delivery and add value.

Why This Book Is Essential

Whether you're new to IT service management or a seasoned professional, this book will furnish you with the knowledge and skills you need to:

- Speak the language of ITIL confidently
- Enhance the quality and efficiency of your IT service delivery
- Align IT with the strategic objectives of your organization
- Create a culture of value co-creation with customers
- Drive continuous improvement in your operations

Let's Get Started!

Are you ready to transform your approach to IT service management? Excellent! The subsequent chapters will delve deeper into the fascinating world of ITIL 4.

Additional Resources

- **Axelos Official ITIL Website:**
  https://www.axelos.com/best-practice-solutions/itil

Unveiling ITIL 4

The world of IT and business is transforming faster than ever, and organizations need to adapt to thrive in this digital era. ITIL 4 provides a powerful toolkit to navigate this continuous evolution and enhance service delivery. In this chapter, we'll delve into the origins of ITIL, explore its evolution to ITIL 4, and outline why it's an essential framework for modern businesses.

The Origins and Evolution of ITIL

- **Humble Beginnings:** ITIL's roots trace back to the UK government in the 1980s, where it emerged as a way to standardize and improve IT processes within government agencies.
- **Global Adoption:** Realizing its inherent value, ITIL gained widespread acceptance across private sectors and other countries, becoming a de-facto standard for IT service management (ITSM).
- **Continuous Refinement:** ITIL has gone through several iterations, reflecting changes in technology and best practices. Earlier versions, like ITIL v3, focused on the IT Service Lifecycle.
- **The Leap to ITIL 4:** ITIL 4 marked a significant shift in 2019, emphasizing customer-centricity, flexibility, and the ability to handle modern technologies like cloud computing, AI, and automation.

What Makes ITIL 4 Different

ITIL 4 brings some key enhancements over its predecessors:

- **Value Co-creation:** ITIL 4 elevates the customer's role, understanding that value is created through active collaboration between service providers and consumers.

- **Holistic Approach:** ITIL 4 promotes a broader view, going beyond IT to embrace all elements of an organization – its culture, people, partners, and processes – that contribute to service delivery.
- **Embrace of Emerging Trends:** ITIL 4 is tailor-made for the digital age, aligning itself seamlessly with Agile, DevOps, and Lean methodologies.
- **Practical Guidance:** ITIL 4 presents actionable frameworks and practices to help organizations see tangible improvements in their service management.

The Building Blocks of ITIL 4

Let's break down the critical components that form the ITIL 4 foundation:

- **The Four Dimensions of Service Management:** ITIL 4 recognizes four crucial dimensions that must work in harmony for successful service delivery. We'll cover these in more detail later.
- **The Service Value System (SVS):** The SVS serves as the heart of ITIL 4, depicting how all elements of an organization work together to generate value for customers.
- **The Guiding Principles:** A set of universal recommendations that guide optimal decision-making and behavior in diverse IT service management scenarios.
- **The Service Value Chain:** A series of activities that transform inputs into valuable outputs, forming the operational core of the ITIL 4 framework.
- **ITIL Practices:** 34 distinct practices that provide structured guidance on various aspects of service management, such as incident management, change enablement, knowledge management, and more.

Why ITIL 4 Matters

In today's business landscape, ITIL 4 is relevant for numerous reasons:

- **Customer Focus:** ITIL 4 helps organizations tailor their services to actual customer needs, improving satisfaction and loyalty.
- **Efficiency and Agility:** It streamlines IT operations, reducing costs and improving adaptability to market changes.
- **Competitive Advantage:** Effective service management enabled by ITIL 4 can set businesses apart and give them an edge in a crowded marketplace.
- **Better Alignment:** ITIL 4 helps foster synergy between IT and other business units, enabling them to work towards unified goals.
- **Risk Management:** ITIL 4 encourages proactive risk identification and mitigation for more reliable service delivery.

Embarking on the ITIL 4 Journey

This book is your stepping-stone into the structured and practical world of ITIL 4. Let's continue the journey and dive deeper into the key concepts of this powerful framework!

Additional Resources

- **Axelos Official ITIL Website:** https://www.axelos.com/best-practice-solutions/itil
- **ITIL Foundation Exam Specifications:** This resource provides insights into the concepts covered in the foundational ITIL 4 exam. https://www.axelos.com/certifications/itil-certifications/itil-foundation-level

Decoding Service Organizations

In the realm of ITIL 4, understanding the nature of service organizations is crucial. They act as the foundation upon which successful service management practices are built. Let's dissect what makes a service organization, its typical roles, and the various ways organizations interact within the service economy.

What is a Service Organization?

At its heart, a service organization exists to provide services to its customers. But what exactly is a 'service'? ITIL 4 defines a service as:

- **A means of enabling value co-creation by facilitating outcomes that customers want to achieve, without the customer having to manage specific costs and risks.**

Let's break this down:

- **Value Co-creation:** The customer and the organization work together to generate value, rather than the organization simply handing something over.
- **Outcomes:** Services are focused on desired results rather than just the delivery of a specific product or tool.
- **Managing Costs and Risks:** The service organization helps customers achieve their goals while minimizing the specific risks and costs associated with managing the service on their own.

Types of Service Organizations

Service organizations come in all shapes and sizes, but generally fall into these categories:

- **Internal Service Providers:** Departments within an organization providing services to other units of the same organization. Example: An internal IT department supporting employees.
- **External Service Providers:** Independent companies offering services to other businesses or the general public. Example: A cloud computing provider.
- **Shared Services Units:** Internal units that service multiple sections of an organization, operating on a cost-recovery basis. Example: A centralized HR department supporting various business units within a large corporation.

Typical Roles of Service Organizations

While specific activities vary depending on the industry, some common roles of service organizations include:

- **Service Provider:** The organization designing, delivering, and managing the service.
- **Service Consumer:** The customer receiving and benefiting from the service.
- **Users:** Individuals within the service consumer organization who utilize the services on a daily basis.

Service Relationships

Service organizations form complex relationships within a broader network. These relationships can involve:

- **Contracts:** Formal agreements defining obligations and expectations between the service provider and consumer.
- **Service Level Agreements (SLAs):** Specific measures of performance and quality agreed upon between the provider and consumer.
- **Collaboration:** Working together to understand needs, co-create solutions, and improve the service over time.

- **Competition:** Sometimes, multiple service organizations offer similar services, creating market competition.

Why Understanding Service Organizations Matters

Grasping the nature of service organizations is an ITIL 4 cornerstone for several reasons:

- **Customer Perspective:** Appreciating the distinct roles of the provider and consumer aids in designing customer-focused services.
- **Optimization:** Understanding service relationships helps streamline processes, reduce friction, and improve the overall service experience.
- **Risk Management:** Recognizing the interconnectedness of service organizations is crucial for identifying and mitigating potential risks across the service landscape.
- **Effective Communication:** Clearly defining roles and responsibilities fosters clear communication channels between service organizations and their stakeholders.

Moving Forward

The concept of service organizations is foundational to mastering ITIL 4. In the next chapter, we will delve further into the ways service organizations interact and explore how to manage these interactions effectively.

Additional Resources:

- **The IT Service Management Forum (itSMF):** An independent organization dedicated to advancing IT service management practices: https://www.itsmfi.org/
- **Service Integration and Management (SIAM):** A field focusing on managing multiple service providers in a complex environment: https://www.siam-foundation.com/

Exploring Service Organizations

In the previous chapter, we defined service organizations and discussed their various roles. Now, let's delve into how these organizations work together in a dynamic environment, exploring the essential aspects for successful interactions within the service economy.

The Service Ecosystem

It's important to see beyond individual service organizations and understand the wider 'service ecosystem' in which they operate. This ecosystem is an interconnected web of multiple organizations, all contributing components to the overarching delivery of a service to an end customer.

Think of it like creating a delicious meal. You have a farmer (growing ingredients), a logistics company (transporting produce), a grocery store (selling the ingredients), and finally, a restaurant chef (preparing the meal for the customer). Each entity is a service organization in its own right, yet they're all part of a broader system focused on the ultimate outcome – a satisfied diner.

Types of Interactions between Service Organizations

- **Collaboration:** In the spirit of value co-creation, service organizations frequently collaborate. This might include sharing knowledge, resources, or aligning processes to achieve mutually beneficial goals.
- **Competition:** Sometimes, organizations offer similar services, creating market competition. While competition can drive innovation and efficiency, it's crucial to maintain healthy relationships between potential rivals.
- **Outsourcing:** When an organization needs specialized skills or capacity, they might outsource parts of their service to an external service provider.

- **Partnership:** Organizations can forge strategic partnerships to complement each other's offerings and expand their reach.

Key Considerations for Managing Service Organizations

To effectively navigate the service ecosystem, here are some essential areas to focus on:

- **Governance:** Clear rules, decision-making structures, and accountability frameworks ensure that the actions of various service organizations are aligned and lead to the desired outcomes.
- **Communication:** Open channels of communication are vital for sharing information, resolving issues, providing timely updates, and ensuring transparency.
- **Contracts and SLAs:** Formal agreements like contracts and Service Level Agreements (SLAs) set clear expectations, define responsibilities, and provide mechanisms for measuring performance.
- **Culture:** A collaborative and customer-focused culture across service organizations fosters smoother interaction and leads to better results for the end consumer.

Tools and Techniques for Managing Interactions

ITIL 4 and other service management frameworks offer several tools and techniques to enhance these interactions:

- **Supplier Management:** A practice focused on managing suppliers and ensuring third-party providers deliver the necessary value.
- **Service Integration and Management (SIAM):** An approach designed to manage multiple service providers effectively within a complex service environment.
- **Stakeholder Management:** Strategies to identify, engage with, and understand the needs of various stakeholders

(customers, users, suppliers, etc.) throughout the service lifecycle.

The Road to Success

Successfully exploring and managing the dynamics of service organizations requires active effort and attention. By prioritizing clear communication, collaboration, a focus on value for the end-user, and utilizing the right tools and techniques, organizations can create successful networks of service providers and exceed customer expectations.

Additional Resources

- **Service Integration and Management (SIAM):** https://www.siam-foundation.com/
- **Supplier Management Processes:** https://www.instituteforsupplymanagement.org/supply-management-competency/supplier-management
- **Stakeholder Management Resources:** https://www.pmi.org/

Section 2:
Mastering Service Management Fundamentals

Navigating the World of Service Management

To effectively implement ITIL 4 principles, it's vital to first develop a solid grasp of the fundamental world of service management. Let's chart our course through this expansive territory, exploring essential definitions, key objectives, and the broader landscape within which ITIL 4 operates.

Defining Key Terms

- **Service:** A means of enabling value co-creation by facilitating outcomes that customers want to achieve, without the customer having to manage specific costs and risks.
- **Product:** A configuration of resources created by an organization that will be potentially valuable for its customers.
- **Service Management:** A set of specialized organizational capabilities for enabling value for customers in the form of services.
- **IT Service Management (ITSM):** The application of service management concepts specifically to IT services, leveraging technology to co-create value with customers.

Understanding the Goals of Service Management

Successful service management has several primary objectives:

- **Value Creation:** At the heart of service management lies the goal of generating real value for both the service provider and the customer.
- **Outcome Focus:** Services are designed to achieve desired outcomes for the customer, not simply deliver an output or component.
- **Efficiency and Effectiveness:** Service management seeks to optimize resource usage, reduce waste, and streamline processes.
- **Customer Satisfaction:** Positive customer experiences, meeting needs and exceeding expectations are critical indicators of success.
- **Risk Management:** Proactively identifying and mitigating potential risks to ensure service reliability and minimize disruption.

The Service Management Spectrum

Service management exists at various levels and interacts with other important management disciplines:

- **Strategic Management:** Service management must align with the overarching goals and strategic direction of the organization.
- **Project Management:** Projects often deliver components or changes that are vital for overall service delivery.
- **Portfolio Management:** Service management encompasses managing the portfolio of services offered to customers.
- **Operations Management:** Day-to-day operations are tightly interwoven with the successful delivery of services.

Trends Shaping Service Management

The world of service management is constantly evolving. Key trends driving change include:

- **Increase in Cloud Services:** The widespread adoption of cloud-based solutions requires a flexible service management approach.
- **DevOps and Agile Methodologies:** Emphasis on collaboration and rapid iterations between development and operations influences service delivery.
- **Automation and AI:** Automation is streamlining tasks, while AI is enhancing decision-making capabilities within service management.
- **Customer Experience (CX):** Increasingly, exceptional customer experiences are becoming a primary differentiator for service organizations.

Significance of ITIL 4

ITIL 4 emerged as a powerful framework within this dynamic service management landscape. It provides structured guidance, best practices, and a common language enabling organizations to:

- Adapt to shifting demands
- Improve efficiency
- Create consistent value for customers
- Foster a culture of collaboration and innovation

Setting the Stage for ITIL 4 Mastery

Understanding the overarching landscape of service management provides a solid foundation for effectively applying ITIL 4 concepts. Let's delve deeper into the heart of service management: the concept of value.

Additional Resources

- **ISACA: Framework for IT governance and control:** https://www.isaca.org/
- **The IT Service Management Forum (itSMF): Devoted to advancing ITSM best practices:** https://www.itsmfi.org/
- **DevOps Institute: Focused on the intersection of DevOps and ITSM:** https://devopsinstitute.com/

Unlocking the Essence of Value

In the realm of service management, the concept of value reigns supreme. Without a clear understanding of value, the creation of impactful services becomes a shot in the dark. Let's explore why value is crucial, how it's defined, and the factors that influence it.

Why Does Value Matter?

Value is the heart and soul of effective service management. Several factors point to its importance:

- **Customer Focus:** Services that don't provide true value to the customer ultimately fail. Understanding value drives customer-centric service design.
- **Decision-Making:** Sound decision-making in service management hinges on a solid grasp of what constitutes value for stakeholders.
- **Resource Optimization:** Value guides the allocation of resources, ensuring they are directed towards initiatives that yield positive outcomes for the customer.
- **Competitive Edge:** Delivering exceptional value sets organizations apart in a crowded marketplace, fostering customer loyalty.

Defining Value

ITIL 4 defines value as: **"The perceived benefits, usefulness, and importance of something."** Key concepts in this definition:

- **Perception:** Value is subjective. What one customer finds valuable, another might not.
- **Benefits:** Value is tied to the positive outcomes and results that the service helps the customer achieve.
- **Usefulness:** Value implies that the service is fit for purpose and solves a real problem or need for the customer.

- **Importance:** Value is relative and reflects the priorities and goals of the customer.

Co-creation of Value

Critically, ITIL 4 emphasizes that value is not something a service provider delivers unilaterally. It is co-created through the active collaboration between the service provider and the service consumer. This collaboration ensures the service is closely aligned with the consumer's specific needs and circumstances.

Factors Influencing Value

Several variables shape the customer's perception of value. These include:

- **Outcomes:** Does the service help the customer achieve their desired objectives?
- **Experiences:** The positive or negative experiences a customer has while interacting with the service.
- **Price and Costs:** The financial aspects, including the price of the service and the underlying costs for the customer to use it.
- **Risks:** Potential risks or negative consequences that the customer might associate with the service.
- **Utility and Warranty:** Is the service fit for purpose (utility) and does it meet agreed-upon conditions (warranty)? We'll delve into these concepts further in Chapter 18.

Determining Value

Since value is highly subjective, how can organizations determine what is considered valuable by their customers? Here are some helpful tools:

- **Customer Feedback:** Direct feedback, surveys, and interviews gather valuable insights into customer perceptions of value.
- **Market Research:** Analyzing trends, competitor offerings, and wider industry data can shed light on what customers value.
- **Outcome tracking:** Measuring the results achieved through service use offers tangible evidence of its value.

Value in the Service Value System

Value plays a central role within the ITIL 4 Service Value System (SVS). The SVS ensures that all components within an organization come together to contribute to value creation for customers. We'll explore this system in-depth later in the book.

Moving Forward

Grasping the nature of value empowers organizations to design and deliver truly impactful services. Our next step is to understand the complex structure and internal workings of the organizations providing these services.

Additional Resources

- **Article: What is Value Co-Creation?** https://hbr.org/
- **Business Value Dashboard Examples:** https://public.tableau.com/en-us/gallery

Delving into Organizations and their Dynamics

Service organizations don't exist in a vacuum. They are complex systems with various internal components, structures, cultures, and people that shape their ability to deliver value to customers. Understanding these dynamics is crucial for effective ITIL 4 implementation.

Elements of an Organization

To grasp how an organization functions, let's dissect its critical elements:

- **Structure:** The formal arrangement of roles, responsibilities, and reporting lines within an organization. This can be hierarchical, flat, matrix-based, or other variations.
- **Culture:** The shared values, beliefs, and norms that guide behavior and decision-making across the organization.
- **People:** The individuals with diverse skills, knowledge, and experiences who contribute to an organization's goals.
- **Processes:** The structured series of activities and workflows that transform inputs into outputs.
- **Technology:** The tools, systems, and infrastructure that facilitate the execution of tasks and service delivery.

How Organizations Function

These elements interact in dynamic ways:

- **Governance:** Organizations establish governance mechanisms to set direction, provide oversight, and ensure alignment between activities and goals.

- **Leadership:** Leaders inspire, guide, and set the tone for the overall culture and direction of the organization.
- **Change Management:** Organizations must adapt to internal and external shifts. Change management processes guide controlled and systematic change.
- **Communication and Collaboration:** Clear lines of communication and collaboration between different units are critical for the seamless flow of information and collective action.

Types of Organizational Structures

Common organizational structures include:

- **Functional:** Organized by specialized skills, like IT, operations, marketing, and finance. This offers efficient specialization but can sometimes result in departmental silos.
- **Hierarchical:** A traditional top-down structure with clear reporting lines and accountability. This offers stability but can be less flexible in dynamic environments.
- **Matrix:** Combines functional and project-based teams. This provides flexibility and adaptability but can create complexity in decision-making.
- **Flat:** Minimizes layers of hierarchy and emphasizes self-management. This offers speed and agility but requires a high degree of responsibility and clear communication.

Influence of Organizational Culture

Organizational culture has a significant bearing on its effectiveness. Let's look at some aspects of culture relevant to service delivery:

- **Customer Centricity:** Does the culture prioritize customer needs and value co-creation?

- **Open Communication:** Does the organization value sharing information and transparency between departments?
- **Collaboration:** Is teamwork encouraged, breaking down silos to achieve shared goals?
- **Innovation:** Does the organization foster a culture of experimentation and learning from failures?
- **Agility:** How quickly can the organization respond to changes in the market or customer needs?

Implications for Service Management

Here's how understanding organizational dynamics impacts ITIL 4 application:

- **Alignment with Structure:** Service management initiatives need to be tailored to the specific organizational structure for optimal outcome.
- **Proactive Change Management:** ITIL 4 changes often involve wider organizational changes. Robust change management practices are crucial.
- **Cultural Considerations:** Service management practices should be designed to foster a customer-centric, collaborative, and agile culture.

Moving Forward

Grasping the internal workings of organizations helps shape a service management approach that is aligned and effective. Next, we'll turn to a critical component of any organization: its people.

Additional Resources

- **Organizational Culture and its Impact:** https://hbr.org/topic/organizational-culture
- **Common Organizational Structures:** https://hbr.org/

- **Organizational Change Management (OCM):** https://www.prosci.com/

Understanding the Human Factor

People are the heartbeat of any organization, and service management is no exception. ITIL 4 explicitly recognizes the vital role that individuals play in service co-creation. Understanding the human element is key for creating positive customer experiences and maximizing organizational efficiency.

Why the Human Factor Matters

The human factor in service management has far-reaching implications:

- **Customer Experience (CX):** The behavior, skills, and attitudes of employees greatly shape the customer's perception of the service they receive.
- **Organizational Culture:** Individuals form the building blocks of an organization's culture. Values, motivation, and communication styles directly influence performance.
- **Innovation and Agility:** Empowered and motivated employees drive innovation and enable organizations to adapt quickly to meet changing demands.
- **Knowledge and Skills:** The collective knowledge, skills, and expertise of employees determine an organization's capacity to provide excellent services.
- **Risk Mitigation:** Human error can be a source of risk. Proactive risk management includes training, awareness, and processes to minimize human-related risks.

Key Aspects of the Human Factor

ITIL 4 emphasizes these key aspects of the human factor in service management:

- **Roles and Responsibilities:** Clearly defined roles and responsibilities empower employees, provide accountability, and ensure the right people are making decisions.
- **Skills and Competencies:** Employees need the necessary skills and knowledge to fulfill their roles effectively. Ongoing training and development are essential.
- **Communication and Collaboration:** Seamless service delivery often requires cross-departmental collaboration. Strong communication channels and skills are critical.
- **Motivation and Employee Engagement:** Motivated employees go the extra mile, fostering a positive work environment and better customer experiences.
- **Leadership:** Leaders play a pivotal role in building a healthy culture, empowering employees, and supporting professional development.

The Challenge of Human Variability

Unlike machines, humans are complex and unpredictable! Here are some challenges that stem from human variability:

- **Inconsistency:** Service quality might fluctuate depending on the individual employee providing the service.
- **Emotional Influences:** Personal feelings, stress, or biases can potentially impact decision-making and customer interactions.
- **Resistance to Change:** Change initiatives can face resistance if employees do not see the value or if they fear the unknown.

ITIL 4 Guidance on Managing the Human Factor

ITIL 4 offers principles and practices to address these challenges:

- **Knowledge Management:** Capturing, sharing, and promoting the use of knowledge empowers employees and reduces dependency on specific individuals.

- **Training and Development:** Continuous investment in skills development enhances service quality and consistency.
- **Change Enablement:** Proactive change management strategies help ease transitions and gain buy-in from employees.
- **Leadership Practices:** Building strong leadership at all levels nurtures a positive culture and fosters employee engagement.
- **Workforce and Talent management:** A specific ITIL 4 practice devoted to strategic human resource considerations in a service management context.

Beyond the Basics

Successful service management goes beyond technical aspects. Consider these additional points:

- **Empathy:** Understanding customer needs and emotions is just as important as technical proficiency.
- **Gamification:** Introducing elements of games into training or work activities can be a fun way to promote engagement and learning.

Continuous Development

Managing the human factor is an ongoing endeavor. Regular evaluations, employee feedback mechanisms, and investment in growth opportunities will enhance the impact of this vital component of service delivery.

Additional Resources

- **Human Resources for IT Professionals:** https://www.shrm.org/
- **The Impact of Employee Engagement:** https://hbr.org/topic/employee-engagement

- **ITIL 4 Workforce and Talent Management Practice Overview:** https://www.beyond20.com/blog/an-overview-of-the-new-itil-4-workforce-and-talent-management-practice/

Crafting Stellar Services and Products

At the heart of successful service management lies the ability to design and deliver services and products that truly meet customer needs and exceed their expectations. This chapter provides a roadmap to achieving this goal, blending theoretical concepts with practical ITIL 4 insights.

The Difference between Services and Products

While often mentioned together, let's clarify the distinction between services and products in the ITIL 4 context:

- **Services:** Intangible means of co-creating value by facilitating desired outcomes for customers, without the customer taking ownership of specific costs and risks.
- **Products:** Tangible or virtual configurations of resources that have the potential to generate value for customers. Products are often components used to deliver a comprehensive service.

The Building Blocks of Stellar Services and Products

Exceptional services and products are built on several key components:

- **Customer Focus:** Deeply understanding your target customers – their needs, pain points, and desired outcomes – is a non-negotiable starting point.
- **Value Proposition:** A clear articulation of why your service or product is uniquely valuable and how it solves a specific problem for the customer.

- **Design Principles:** Employ human-centered design thinking to create intuitive, user-friendly services and products.
- **Features and Functionality:** Deliver features that directly align with customer needs, avoiding bloat or unnecessary complexity.
- **Quality and Reliability:** Strive for high quality and consistent performance to build trust in your offerings.
- **Support and Maintenance:** Provide accessible resources, channels, and timely fixes to ensure the continuous value creation of your services and products.

Service and Product Design in ITIL 4

ITIL 4 emphasizes a structured approach to crafting services and products:

- **Service Design Practice:** A practice focused on the design of new or changed services. It encompasses the key building blocks we just discussed.
- **The Service Value Chain:** The SVS includes 'design and transition' activities, ensuring new offerings integrate seamlessly with the broader service ecosystem.
- **Continual Improvement:** Regularly gather customer feedback and analyze performance data to drive ongoing improvements to your services and products.

Tools and Techniques

Let's look at some helpful tools and methods for stellar design:

- **Customer Journey Mapping:** Visualize customers' experiences across various touchpoints with your service to identify pain points and improvement opportunities.
- **Personas:** Create fictional customer profiles to represent your target audience and guide design decisions.

- **Prototyping and Testing:** Develop quick, low-cost prototypes for early feedback and iteration to refine your service or product.
- **Minimum Viable Product (MVP):** A barebones version of your offering with core functionality, ideal for gathering user feedback in a real-world context.

Key Considerations

In addition to design principles, these points are crucial for success:

- **Scalability:** Plan for growth. Does your design allow for increased usage?
- **Security:** Address security risks proactively with robust protocols.
- **Regulatory Compliance:** Ensure your services and products adhere to relevant regulations and industry standards.
- **Accessibility:** Design with inclusivity in mind, ensuring users with various abilities can enjoy your offerings.

The Role of Technology

In today's landscape, technology is an integral part of service and product design. Consider these aspects:

- **Automation:** Automate repetitive tasks to improve efficiency and free up resources for innovation.
- **Cloud Technologies:** Leverage the flexibility and scalability of cloud computing for service delivery and product development.
- **Data and Analytics:** Utilize data insights to refine your services and products and personalize customer experiences.

Crafting Excellence

Building truly exceptional services and products is a continuous endeavor. By embracing customer-centricity, employing design thinking, utilizing ITIL 4 principles, and iterating continuously, you'll consistently deliver offerings that drive value and foster customer loyalty.

Additional Resources

- **Service Design Tools and Techniques:**
  https://www.servicedesigntools.org/
- **Human-Centered Design Overview:**
  https://www.interaction-design.org/literature/topics/human-centered-design
- **Minimum Viable Product (MVP) resources:**
  https://www.productplan.com/glossary/minimum-viable-product/

Shaping Service Offerings for Success

Designing excellent services and products (as explored in the previous chapter) is only one piece of the puzzle. To truly succeed, you must carefully craft and package your offerings to align with your customers' needs and effectively communicate their unique value.

What is a Service Offering?

ITIL 4 defines a service offering as: **"A description of one or more services, designed to address the needs of a target consumer group. A service offering may include goods, access to resources, and service actions."**

Let's dissect this definition:

- **Focus on Specific Needs:** Service offerings target defined customer segments and solve particular problems or achieve specific outcomes.
- **Combination of Elements:** They bundle together the right services, products, resources, and necessary actions for a comprehensive solution.

Types of Service Offerings

Here are common types of service offerings you might encounter:

- **Core Offerings:** The fundamental services representing the heart of your value proposition.
- **Packaged Offerings:** Bundles of several services or products targeted for a specific customer need or industry.

- **Tiered Offerings:** Variations of a service offered at different levels (e.g., basic, premium) with varying features and pricing.
- **Customized Offerings:** Tailored offerings designed for specific clients with unique requirements.

Strategic Alignment

Shaping successful service offerings requires alignment with the overall business strategy and understanding of the competitive landscape:

- **Organizational Goals:** Service offerings should support broader business objectives, such as expansion into new markets or revenue growth.
- **Market Analysis:** Research competitor offerings and understand the specific needs and pain points of your target customers.
- **Differentiation:** Identify what makes your services unique and desirable. Articulate your value proposition clearly.

Key Components of Service Offerings

Effective service offerings typically include the following components:

- **Service Description:** A clear overview of what the service entails, the benefits it delivers, and the outcomes it helps customers achieve.
- **Target Audience:** Define your ideal customer and their specific needs.
- **Pricing and Contract Terms:** Establish transparent pricing models, billing processes, and Service Level Agreements (SLAs) that define performance expectations.
- **Support and Maintenance:** Specify support channels, response times, and escalation procedures to provide customers with continuous support.

- **Service Levels:** Differentiate between standard and premium service levels if you offer tiered options.

Lifecycle Management

Service offerings evolve over time. ITIL 4 emphasizes the following stages in their lifecycle:

- **Design:** Design new offerings guided by customer insights and organizational goals.
- **Introduction:** Launch offerings with well-defined marketing and communication efforts.
- **Management:** Monitor usage, gather feedback, and refine offerings through continual improvement.
- **Retirement:** Decommission outdated offerings when they no longer align with market needs or business strategies.

Tools and Techniques

Shaping successful service offerings involves:

- **Market Research:** Collect market data (surveys, competitor analysis, etc.) to understand customer needs and industry trends.
- **Service Portfolio Management:** A practice that ensures that the organization has the right mix of services to meet strategic objectives.
- **Financial Management:** Assess profitability, identify costs associated with delivering the offering, and set appropriate pricing models.
- **Marketing and Communication:** Develop compelling messaging to highlight the value proposition and reach the target audience.

The Art of Value Articulation

Convincing customers of your offering's worth is critical. Focus on these key aspects:

- **Outcomes not Features:** Emphasize the results customers will achieve rather than just listing technical capabilities.
- **Success Stories and Testimonials:** Showcase tangible evidence of how you've helped other customers to build credibility.
- **Clarity and Simplicity:** Avoid jargon and complex language. Make your offerings easy to understand.

Continuous Improvement

The marketplace is dynamic! Regularly monitor the performance of your service offerings and seek to improve them through:

- **Customer Feedback:** Gather feedback through surveys, reviews, and direct communication to identify areas for refinement.
- **Monitoring KPIs:** Track Key Performance Indicators (KPIs) aligned with your business objectives and service metrics.

Additional Resources

- **ITIL 4 Service Portfolio Management Practice Overview:** https://www.axelos.com/best-practice-solutions/itil
- **Marketing Service Offerings:** https://blog.hubspot.com/service/service-marketing-strategies]

Ready to build strong connections and cultivate fruitful relationships with your customers? Let's explore that in the next chapter!

Cultivating Fruitful Service Relationships

Exceptional service delivery is built upon strong relationships between service providers, consumers, and users. Nurturing these relationships is essential for maximizing value creation, fostering collaboration, and enhancing the overall service experience.

Why Service Relationships Matter

Here's why prioritizing service relationships is paramount:

- **Value Co-creation:** Strong relationships facilitate knowledge sharing, collaboration, and alignment of objectives, enabling the co-creation of greater value for all parties.
- **Proactive Problem Solving:** Open communication channels promote transparency and the ability to address issues quickly and effectively before they escalate.
- **Trust and Loyalty:** Positive relationships foster trust, encouraging customers to return and leading to long-term, mutually beneficial partnerships.
- **Innovation:** Healthy partnerships pave the way for joint brainstorming and experimentation, driving innovation.
- **Enhanced Customer Satisfaction:** Customers who feel valued and heard are more likely to be satisfied with the service experience.

Stakeholders in Service Relationships

Effective service relationship management involves understanding the diverse stakeholders and their roles:

- **Service Provider:** The organization designing and delivering the service.

- **Service Consumer:** The organization or entity receiving the service.
- **Users:** Individual people within the service consumer organization who utilize the service in their day-to-day activities.
- **Suppliers:** External organizations providing goods or services essential to the service provider.
- **Partners:** Organizations collaborating with the service provider for mutual benefit.

Building Strong Service Relationships

Here's how to cultivate positive and enduring service relationships:

- **Clear Communication:** Establish open communication channels, provide regular updates, and foster a transparent environment.
- **Trust and Respect:** Act with integrity, fulfill promises, and treat all stakeholders with respect.
- **Shared Goals:** Ensure alignment between the service provider and consumer's expectations and work towards mutually beneficial outcomes.
- **Customer Focus:** Put the needs of customers and users at the forefront of decision-making and service design.
- **Conflict Resolution:** Implement mechanisms to handle disagreements proactively and fairly, aiming for win-win situations.

ITIL 4 Practices for Relationship Management

ITIL 4 offers specific practices to support building healthy service relationships:

- **Service Level Management:** Focuses on defining, monitoring, and managing service levels agreed upon in Service Level Agreements (SLAs), forming the foundation of clear expectations.

- **Supplier Management:** Ensures suppliers meet their contractual obligations and contribute to the delivery of quality services.
- **Business Relationship Management (BRM):** A strategic practice that fosters strong, long-lasting connections with service consumers, focusing on understanding their business needs and goals.

Tips for Success

Additional pointers for nurturing strong service relationships:

- **Account Management:** Dedicate account managers who act as a single point of contact for key customers.
- **Customer-Centric Culture:** Encourage a customer-obsessed mindset across the organization.
- **Embrace Feedback:** Actively solicit feedback and use it constructively to improve services and strengthen relationships.
- **Measure and Analyze:** Track relevant metrics (customer satisfaction scores, survey results, retention rates) to assess the health of service relationships.

The Role of Technology

Technology plays a crucial role in maintaining strong service relationships:

- **CRM Systems:** Manage customer data, track interactions, and provide valuable insights.
- **Collaboration Platforms:** Facilitate seamless communication and information sharing between stakeholders.
- **Self-Service Portals:** Allow customers to access resources, track requests, and obtain support independently.

Beyond the Basics

Successful service relationships go beyond contractual obligations. Consider:

- **Proactive Engagement:** Anticipate customer needs and proactively offer solutions rather than just reacting to problems.
- **Personalized Experiences:** Leverage customer data to tailor service interactions and offerings.

Continuous Nurturing

Building fruitful service relationships is an ongoing process. Remember, the commitment to fostering strong relationships will reap rewards in the form of enhanced customer satisfaction, long-term loyalty, and mutual value creation.

Additional Resources

- **ITIL 4 Business Relationship Management (BRM):** https://www.axelos.com/best-practice-solutions/itil
- **Customer Relationship Management (CRM) Systems Overview:** https://www.salesforce.com/crm/what-is-crm/

Fostering Connections for Service Excellence

In the previous chapter, we discussed the importance of service relationships. In this chapter, we'll take a broader view, focusing on how to establish strong connections throughout the service ecosystem to optimize service delivery and achieve exceptional results.

The Power of Connections

Successful service management hinges on interconnectivity. A well-connected service ecosystem leads to:

- **Flow of Information:** Seamless communication channels facilitate the exchange of knowledge, requirements, and updates.
- **Collaboration:** Connected teams can work synergistically to solve complex challenges, innovate faster, and provide better outcomes for customers.
- **Reduced Friction:** Efficient handoffs and clear communication across teams reduce bottlenecks and delays, enhancing the overall service experience.
- **Resource Optimization:** Connected organizations share resources, capabilities, and knowledge, enabling them to serve customers more holistically.
- **Agility and Resilience:** A connected ecosystem can adapt quickly to shifting customer needs, disruptions, and market changes.

Building Blocks of Connectivity

Here are crucial components to fostering a connected environment:

- **Shared Culture:** A collaborative working environment where teams value transparency, teamwork, and a shared focus on customer outcomes.
- **Communication Protocols:** Establish clear guidelines on how and when to communicate updates, escalate issues, and engage stakeholders.
- **Knowledge Management:** Capturing and sharing insights, best practices, and lessons learned across the service network empowers everyone involved.
- **Governance Frameworks:** Define how decisions are made, who has authority over specific processes, and how to ensure accountability.
- **Integration Tools:** Use technology to automate information exchange, streamline workflows, and connect disparate teams and systems.

Key Relationships to Nurture

Focus on building strong connections within various relationships:

- **Internal Teams:** Bridge silos between IT, operations, development, and other departments to ensure everyone works towards unified goals.
- **Suppliers and Partners:** Foster collaborative partnerships built on shared goals and mutual respect.
- **Customers:** Maintain open and ongoing communication channels to understand evolving customer needs and expectations.
- **Industry Networks:** Participate in broader industry or professional networks to share knowledge, learn from peers, and benchmark performance.

ITIL 4 Practices Supporting Connectivity

Several ITIL 4 practices are directly focused on building strong connections:

- **Relationship Management:** A general practice dedicated to fostering strong relationships with all types of stakeholders.
- **Supplier Management:** Ensures suppliers deliver on their obligations, contribute to service quality, and have strong relationships with the service provider.
- **Service Integration and Management (SIAM):** A practice focused on the strategic management of multiple service providers to deliver a seamless service experience for customers.

Tips for Success

Here are some additional pointers for enhancing connectivity:

- **Define Roles and Responsibilities:** Clearly outline who does what and who owns specific interactions to minimize confusion and duplication of effort.
- **Visualize Your Ecosystem:** Use diagrams or flowcharts to map dependencies and communication pathways, helping everyone visualize the interconnectedness.
- **Regular Reviews:** Conduct periodic assessments of connection health across your ecosystem. Identify areas for improvement and bottlenecks.

Technology as an Enabler

Technology plays a vital role in fostering connectivity:

- **Collaboration Tools:** Leverage tools for real-time communication, document sharing, and project management to facilitate team alignment.
- **Enterprise Systems:** Systems like ERPs (Enterprise Resource Planning) and CRMs (Customer Relationship Management) provide a shared view of data and processes.

- **APIs and Integrations:** Allow diverse systems and services to 'talk' to each other, promoting data flow and automation.

Cultivating a Collaborative Mindset

Technical connections are essential, but a truly connected ecosystem requires a collaborative mindset. Encourage:

- **Empathy:** Understand the perspectives of various stakeholders, both internal and external.
- **Proactive Engagement:** Encourage proactive information sharing and cooperation.
- **Focus on Shared Goals:** Reinforce that everyone is working towards the bigger picture of delivering value to customers.

Benefits of a Connected Ecosystem

Building a connected service ecosystem translates into tangible outcomes:

- **Enhanced Customer Experience**
- **Increased Innovation**
- **Reduced Costs and Improved Efficiency**
- **Greater Agility and Resilience**

Additional Resources

- **Service Integration and Management (SIAM) Resources:** https://www.scopism.com/siam-foundation/
- **Collaboration Tools for Service Teams:** https://www.g2.com/categories/collaboration

Achieving Desired Outcomes

The ultimate objective of service management is to facilitate the outcomes that customers want to achieve. This chapter examines how to make this a reality, ensuring your services generate tangible value.

What are Outcomes?

ITIL 4 defines an outcome as: **"A result for a stakeholder enabled by one or more outputs."**

Key insights from this definition:

- **Customer-Centric:** Outcomes are about what the customer accomplishes or gains from using the service, not just the service's features.
- **Results-Oriented:** Focus on the change, benefit, or value the customer experience due to the service.
- **Requires Outputs:** Outcomes rely on the service outputs (deliverables, components, or actions performed) but go beyond them.

Examples of Outcomes

Let's illustrate the difference between outputs and outcomes:

- **IT Helpdesk Service:**
    - Output: A resolved incident.
    - Outcome: An employee able to resume work with minimal disruption.
- **Website Hosting Service:**
    - Output: A functioning website.
    - Outcome: Increased online sales for a business.
- **Training Service:**
    - Output: A completed training course.

○ Outcome: Employees with new skills, leading to improved productivity.

Why Focusing on Outcomes Matters

Shifting your attention from outputs to outcomes yields profound benefits:

- **Customer Value:** Helps you design services focused on helping the customer achieve their goals.
- **Strategic Alignment:** Ensures services directly contribute to the customer's broader business objectives.
- **Enhanced Decision-Making:** Guides prioritization of resources and investments by focusing on what delivers the most value.
- **Clearer Measurement:** Provides a framework to define meaningful metrics tied to customer success.

Key Elements for Achieving Outcomes

Here's how to ensure your services enable desired outcomes:

- **Customer Understanding:** Deeply understand your customers – their needs, pain points, and what success means for them.
- **Outcome Definition:** Work with your customers to clearly articulate the specific outcomes the service should help them achieve.
- **Collaboration:** Actively involve customers in the service design and delivery process.
- **Performance Tracking:** Define and track metrics (KPIs) that align with customer outcomes.
- **Feedback Loops:** Continuously gather feedback to assess whether the services lead to the desired results.
- **Adaptability:** Adjust your services based on customer feedback and changes in their desired outcomes.

The Role of Value Co-Creation

True outcome achievement is a collaborative process. Emphasize:

- **Two-Way Communication:** Encourage open dialogue on progress and challenges.
- **Joint Responsibility:** Both service provider and consumer have a role to play in achieving the agreed-upon outcomes.
- **Shared Knowledge:** Share insights about how the service is being used, offering opportunities to optimize it for greater value.

ITIL 4 and Outcome-Driven Service Management

ITIL 4's emphasis on value co-creation naturally aligns with prioritizing outcomes. Here's how:

- **The Service Value System (SVS):** Designed to ensure all components of a service organization contribute to value creation, with outcomes at the heart.
- **Continual Improvement Practice:** Encourages proactive, data-driven iteration and refinement to maximize the outcomes your services deliver.
- **Guiding Principles:** ITIL 4 principles like "Focus on Value" and " Collaborate and Promote Transparency" intrinsically support an outcome-oriented approach.

The Big Picture

Achieving desired outcomes is a dynamic endeavor. Customer needs evolve over time. Stay flexible and maintain ongoing communication to ensure your services remain relevant.

Additional Resources

- **Outcomes vs. Outputs:**
  https://ssir.org/articles/entry/understanding_the_difference_
  between_outputs_and_outcomes
- **Measuring Outcomes in IT Service Management**
  https://www.axelos.com/certifications/itil-certifications/itil-dir
  ect-plan-improve-module

Realizing Results: The Outcome Continuum

In the previous chapter, we discussed the importance of focusing on desired outcomes. However, the story doesn't end there. Services need to translate outcomes into tangible results that deliver value for both the customer and the service provider. Let's explore how to make this happen.

Understanding the Outcome Continuum

The outcome continuum outlines the progression from service provision to the ultimate realization of value:

1. **Service Outputs:** The direct deliverables of a service (e.g., a working website, a resolved ticket).
2. **Outcomes:** The changes or benefits experienced by the customer due to utilizing the service (e.g., increased website traffic, employee back at work).
3. **Value:** The perceived benefits, usefulness, and importance of the outcomes from the customer's perspective (e.g., increased profit from online sales, higher employee satisfaction).

Why the Outcome Continuum Matters

Focusing on the entire continuum is crucial for:

- **Demonstrating ROI:** Provides a clear articulation of service value, justifying investments and demonstrating return on investment.
- **Guiding Improvements:** Identifying bottlenecks in the outcome continuum illuminates where to optimize service delivery for better results.

- **Building Trust:** Transparency about results earned from services is essential for building long-term partnerships and fostering customer loyalty.

Measuring Results

To track your progress along the outcome continuum, you need to measure and quantify results. Here's how:

- **Define Success Metrics (KPIs):** Select relevant Key Performance Indicators (KPIs) that align with outcomes and desired value for the customer.
- **Baseline Data:** Capture metrics before service implementation to provide a reference point to measure against.
- **Data Collection:** Implement methods to gather data (surveys, usage analytics, financial tracking, etc.)
- **Analysis and Reporting:** Analyze collected data regularly, visualizing trends and identifying areas for improvement.

Types of Value Realization

The specific type of value achieved will depend on the nature of the service and the goals of the customer. Value can manifest in several ways:

- **Financial:** Increased revenue, reduced costs, and improved profitability.
- **Operational:** Improved efficiency, reduced downtime, and better resource allocation.
- **Customer Experience:** Enhanced customer satisfaction, loyalty, and increased ease of doing business.
- **Strategic Alignment:** Supporting the customer's broader business objectives and competitive advantage.
- **Innovation:** Generating new ideas, products, or business models.

Barriers to Value Realization

Several factors can hinder value realization:

- **Unclear Outcome Definition:** Vaguely defined outcomes make it difficult to measure success.
- **Mismatched Expectations:** Misunderstandings between the service provider and the consumer about intended results.
- **Data Challenges:** Lack of reliable data or difficulty collecting relevant metrics.
- **Resistance to Change:** Users might be resistant to adopting new services or ways of working.
- **External Factors:** Market shifts, economic downturns, or unforeseen events can affect value realization.

Tips for Success

Here are practical strategies to enhance value realization:

- **Iterative Approach:** Regularly assess progress, adjust targets, and refine your services based on data and feedback.
- **Communicate Value:** Effectively communicate realized value to customers and stakeholders, building confidence and trust.
- **Celebrate Successes:** Recognize and celebrate milestones along the outcome continuum to reinforce positive momentum.
- **Accountability:** Establish clear ownership of outcomes and value realization initiatives.

The Role of ITIL 4

ITIL 4 explicitly promotes an outcome-oriented approach, fostering value realization through:

- **Guiding Principles:** Emphasizing customer focus, value co-creation, and continual improvement.
- **Service Value Chain:** Ensuring activities throughout the chain create value for stakeholders.
- **Practices:** ITIL 4 practices like Measurement and Reporting support tracking progress and demonstrating value.

A Value-Driven Mindset

Realizing results is about more than just metrics. Cultivate a mindset that:

- **Prioritizes Value:** Make the pursuit of tangible customer benefits a core priority.
- **Encourages Collaboration:** Facilitate strong collaboration with customers to celebrate joint successes.

Additional Resources

- **Measuring Value Realization in ITSM:** https://www.axiossystems.com/blog/value-realization-it-service-management
- **Best Practices for Demonstrating ROI from Services** https://itsm.tools/demonstrating-roi-service-management-initiatives/

Ready to move onto the next fundamental concept—understanding the costs associated with service management?

Demystifying Costs in Service Management

While focused on value creation, effective service management necessitates a keen understanding of the costs involved. Ignoring costs can lead to financial strain, unsustainable services, and an inability to make informed choices. Let's demystify this crucial component.

Why Cost Management Matters

Effective cost management in service management is essential because it:

- **Enables Informed Decision-Making:** Understanding costs empowers you to make trade-offs between different service designs, optimize resource allocation, and identify areas for cost reduction.
- **Supports Pricing Strategies:** Accurate cost information aids in determining profitable and competitive pricing models for your service offerings.
- **Drives Efficiency:** Visibility into costs pinpoints inefficiencies and wasteful processes, fostering continuous improvement.
- **Ensures Financial Sustainability:** By aligning costs with value creation, you ensure the long-term sustainability and affordability of your services.

Types of Costs in Service Management

Several types of costs are associated with delivering services:

- **Direct Costs:** Costs explicitly linked to a specific service. Includes:
    - People (salaries, benefits)

- Technology (hardware, software, licensing)
- Infrastructure (facilities, data centers)
- Third-party suppliers and vendors
- **Indirect Costs:** Costs shared across multiple services or not easily traceable to a specific service:
  - Overhead (management, finance, HR functions)
  - Amortization of fixed assets (spread capital investments over time)
- **Fixed Costs:** Costs that remain relatively stable regardless of service usage.
- **Variable Costs:** Costs that fluctuate in proportion to service usage.
- **Capital Expenditure (CapEx):** Large upfront investments in assets like infrastructure and hardware.
- **Operational Expenditure (OpEx):** Recurring costs incurred for day-to-day operations such as salaries and maintenance.

Key Principles of Cost Management

Here are some cornerstone principles for effective cost management:

- **Transparency:** Maintain clear, open communication about costs involved with all stakeholders.
- **Value Focus:** Prioritize costs that generate direct customer value, scrutinizing those that do not.
- **Accountability:** Define clear ownership and responsibility for managing costs at different service levels.
- **Total Cost of Ownership (TCO):** Consider the entire cost lifecycle of a service, not just initial investments.
- **Continual Improvement:** Regularly analyze cost data to identify opportunities for optimization.

ITIL 4 and Cost Management

ITIL 4 provides guidance on cost management through:

- **Financial Management Practice:** Focuses on budgeting, accounting, and charging for IT services.
- **Service Value Chain Activities:** Encourages the consideration of cost implications throughout the value chain, from planning to operation.
- **The "Focus on Value" Guiding Principle:** Stresses striking the balance between benefits, costs, and risks in decision-making.

Tools and Techniques

Let's look at tools to help with cost management:

- **Cost Accounting:** Systems and methods for tracking, allocating, and analyzing costs.
- **Cost Modeling:** Creating models to simulate different service scenarios and their financial implications.
- **Benchmarking:** Comparing your costs with industry averages or similar organizations for insight.
- **Activity-Based Costing (ABC):** Assigns costs to activities, revealing where value is created and resources are consumed.

Beyond Pure Numbers

Effective cost management extends beyond simple accounting:

- **Waste Reduction:** Embrace methodologies like Lean ITSM to streamline processes and reduce waste.
- **Opportunity Costs:** Consider 'hidden' costs of not pursuing a project due to current spending.
- **Cost of Risk:** Factor in the potential costs associated with risks when making service management decisions.

The Art of Balancing Costs and Value

Mastering cost management is about striking the right balance between value delivery and efficient resource utilization. Avoid excessive cost-cutting that could endanger service quality and ultimately damage customer value.

Additional Resources

- **Financial Management in IT Service Management:** https://www.axelos.com/best-practice-solutions/itil/what-is-itil/itil-glossary/it-financial-management
- **Cost Accounting Guide:** https://corporatefinanceinstitute.com/resources/knowledge/accounting/cost-accounting/
- **Total Cost of Ownership (TCO) in IT** https://www.gartner.com/en/information-technology/glossary/total-cost-of-ownership-tco

Ready to explore how to proactively mitigate risks in service management?

Mitigating Risks: A Comprehensive Approach

Service management thrives in a stable environment, but the reality is that services are exposed to risks. These risks can jeopardize value, disrupt operations, and damage reputation. A proactive risk management approach is essential for minimizing negative surprises and ensuring continuity.

What is Risk in Service Management?

ITIL 4 defines risk as: **"A possible event that could cause harm or loss, or make it more difficult to achieve objectives."**

Let's break this down:

- **Possible Event:** Risk refers to something that might happen, but hasn't occurred yet.
- **Harm or Loss:** Risks threaten value creation, objectives, or the well-being of stakeholders.
- **Uncertainty:** The outcome of a risk is not guaranteed.

Types of Risks

Service organizations encounter a range of risks:

- **Operational Risks:** Disruptions to daily operations, such as system outages, security breaches, or supplier failures.
- **Strategic Risks:** Threats to the organization's long-term goals, like changing economic conditions or new competitors.
- **Project Risks:** Risks associated with delivering change initiatives or new services.
- **Financial Risks:** Issues related to budgets, inaccurate cost estimations, or financial instability.

- **Compliance Risks:** Failure to adhere to relevant laws, regulations, or industry standards.
- **Reputational Risks:** Events that can damage the organization's reputation or erode customer trust.
- **Human-Related Risks:** Errors, absenteeism, or lack of necessary skills within the workforce.
- **Environmental Risks:** Natural disasters, climate change, or infrastructure failures.

Risk Management Fundamentals

Effective risk management involves these core components:

- **Risk Identification:** Proactively uncovering potential risks through brainstorming, scenario analysis, and reviewing historical data.
- **Risk Analysis:** Evaluating the likelihood and impact of each identified risk to prioritize responses.
- **Risk Response:** Developing strategies to address risks:
  - Mitigate (reduce the probability or impact)
  - Transfer (share the risk with a third-party)
  - Avoid (eliminate the activity causing the risk)
  - Accept (take no action if risk is minor or unavoidable)
- **Risk Monitoring and Control:** Regularly reviewing risk status, updating plans, and identifying emerging risks.

ITIL 4 and Risk Management

ITIL 4 emphasizes integrated risk management practices:

- **Risk Management Practice:** A dedicated ITIL 4 practice focusing on establishing and maintaining an effective risk management approach.
- **The "Optimize and Automate" Guiding Principle:** Encourages automation to reduce human error and risks associated with manual processes.

- **The Service Value Chain:** Risk considerations should be embedded within each activity across the value chain.

Tools and Techniques

- **Risk Register:** A document to capture identified risks, their assessment, and response plans
- **SWOT Analysis:** A strategic tool to identify Strengths, Weaknesses, Opportunities, and Threats to the organization or service.
- **Probability and Impact Matrix:** Used to visualize and prioritize risks based on their likelihood and severity.
- **Failure Mode and Effect Analysis (FMEA):** A method to proactively anticipate failure points and devise preventive measures.

Building a Risk-Aware Culture

Risk management isn't just about policies. Here's how to embed it into your culture:

- **Leadership Support:** Leaders model risk-conscious decision-making and set the tone for the organization.
- **Transparency:** Encourage open communication about risks and avoid a culture of blame.
- **Resilience:** Foster a mindset that embraces learning from failures and adapting in the face of uncertainty.

A Note on Opportunity

While primarily focused on mitigating threats, risk management also relates to opportunities. Proactively seek out potential upsides!

Additional Resources

- **ITIL 4 Risk Management Practice Overview:**
  https://www.axelos.com/best-practice-solutions/itil/itil-4
- **Risk Management Best Practices:**
  https://www.pmi.org/learning/library/risk-management-best-practices-8814
- **ISO 31000: Risk Management Standard**
  https://www.iso.org/standard/72140.html

Safeguarding Operations: Strategies for Risk Management

In the previous chapter, we discussed a comprehensive approach to risk management. Now, we focus on fortifying your operations against disruptions and ensuring they are reliable and secure.

Why Operational Risk Matters

Operational risks are the most common threats, potentially leading to:

- **Service Downtime:** Negative impacts customer experience, productivity, and revenue.
- **Data Breaches:** Loss of sensitive information, reputational damage, and legal consequences.
- **Missed SLAs:** Breaching contract agreements, incurring penalties, and straining customer relationships.
- **Loss of Productivity:** Disruptions causing employees and teams to lose valuable time.
- **Increased Costs:** Remediation actions after incidents can be resource-intensive and costly.

Key Areas of Operational Risk

Let's dissect common areas where operational risks arise:

- **Infrastructure Failures:** Hardware, network, or data center outages can cripple service delivery.
- **Security Vulnerabilities:** Cybersecurity threats such as malware, ransomware, or unauthorized access.
- **Process Breakdowns:** Errors in manual execution, inadequate procedures, or bottlenecks in workflows.
- **Lack of Capacity:** Insufficient resources to handle service demand, particularly during peak times.

- **Natural Disasters and External Events:** Unpredictable events like extreme weather or power outages can cause disruptions.
- **Human Error:** Mistakes, lack of training, or intentional wrongdoing by employees and third-parties.

Operational Resilience Strategies

Here's how to fortify your operations:

1. **Reliability Engineering:** Design services with resilience in mind, anticipating and preventing potential failure points.
2. **Redundancy and Fault Tolerance:** Deploy backup systems, diverse network paths, and failover mechanisms to minimize single points of failure.
3. **Robust Security Measures:** Implement firewalls, encryption, access control, and vulnerability scanning to safeguard data and systems.
4. **Incident Management:** Have well-defined processes for rapid incident detection, response, and recovery to minimize downtime.
5. **Problem Management:** Proactively analyze recurring incidents to identify and address root causes, preventing future disruptions.
6. **Change Enablement:** Implement rigorous change management processes to reduce the risk of unintended consequences during service updates or modifications.
7. **Disaster Recovery Planning:** Establish plans for recovering critical systems and data in the event of major disruptions or disasters.
8. **Testing and Monitoring:** Regularly test backup systems, disaster recovery plans, and monitor service health for early threat detection.

ITIL 4 Practices for Operational Resilience

ITIL 4 emphasizes operational stability through several practices:

- **Incident Management:** Swiftly restore normal service operation during disruptions.
- **Problem Management:** Identify and address the root causes of recurring incidents.
- **Change Enablement:** Manage changes in a controlled manner to minimize negative impact.
- **Deployment Management:** Ensure smooth transitions of new or changed services into the live environment.
- **Monitoring and Event Management:** Proactive monitoring of systems and services to detect potential issues.

Technology as an Enabler

Technology is crucial to safeguard operations:

- **Automation:** Automate routine tasks and processes to reduce the risk of human error and free up resources.
- **Self-healing Systems:** Introduce systems that can automatically detect and repair issues, minimizing the need for manual intervention.
- **AIOps:** Using Artificial Intelligence for improved monitoring, anomaly detection, and incident response.
- **Cloud-Based Solutions:** Leverage the scalability, resilience, and built-in security features of cloud services.

Building a Resilient Mindset

Operational resilience goes beyond processes and tools, here's how to instill the right mindset:

- **Plan for the Unexpected:** Assume disruptions will happen regardless of precautions and prepare accordingly.
- **Proactive Approach:** Encourage a culture of preventative maintenance and continuous scanning for potential vulnerabilities.

- **Learning from Failure:** Treat incidents as valuable opportunities to learn and improve, avoiding a culture of blame.

Additional Resources

- **ITIL 4 Incident Management Practice:** https://www.axelos.com/best-practice-solutions/itil/itil-4-framework
- **Business Continuity Planning Resources:** https://www.ready.gov/business-continuity-planning-suite
- **Disaster Recovery Best Practices:** https://searchdisasterrecovery.techtarget.com/feature/Disaster-recovery-best-practices

Let's move onto the final pillar in our fundamental concepts – exploring "utility" and "warranty"!

Ensuring Utility and Warranty: The Backbone of Service Value

Every service exists for a reason – to bring value to its users. Utility and warranty are the essential elements that ensure a service fulfills its purpose and meets user expectations.

What is Utility?

ITIL 4 defines utility as: **"The functionality offered by a product or service to meet a particular need."** We can also say it's the fit-for-purpose aspect of the service.

Key points about utility:

- **Customer-Driven:** Utility is determined from the customer's perspective.
- **Functionality:** Does the service provide the capabilities and features users require to achieve their desired outcomes?
- **Removing Constraints:** Utility can be about removing limitations or obstacles that impede the customer.

Examples of Utility

- **Cloud Storage Service:** Utility lies in providing accessible, secure, and reliable storage for customer's data.
- **Training Course:** Utility is gained from the actual knowledge and skills the course imparts.
- **Helpdesk Service:** Utility is in its ability to quickly resolve issues, restoring a user's ability to work.

What is Warranty?

ITIL 4 defines warranty as: **"Assurance that a product or service will meet agreed requirements."** Put simply, it's the fit-for-use aspect of the service.

Key points about warranty:

- **Agreed Requirements:** Warranty is about meeting predefined conditions, typically around performance, availability, security, and capacity.
- **Reliability:** The service functions consistently within agreed-upon parameters.
- **Trust:** Warranty builds confidence in the service, assuring users it will function as promised.

Examples of Warranty

- **Cloud Storage Service:** Warranty includes uptime guarantees (e.g., 99.99% monthly uptime), data protection, and security standards.
- **Internet Service Provider:** Warranty could cover minimum download/upload speeds, maximum latency, and availability commitments.
- **Software as a Service (SaaS):** Warranty might address response times, bug fixes, and adherence to data privacy regulations.

Utility vs. Warranty

While related, there's a subtle difference:

- **Utility:** Is the service fundamentally designed to do what the customer needs?
- **Warranty:** Does the service perform reliably and meet the agreed-upon terms of the service, such as availability and performance?

A service needs BOTH utility and warranty to create value.

Ensuring Utility and Warranty

Here's how to prioritize these crucial aspects:

1. **Understand User Needs:** Deeply understand your users' pain points, requirements, and what success looks like for them.
2. **Define SLAs:** Clearly outline the levels of performance, availability, security, and other relevant factors within Service Level Agreements (SLAs).
3. **Design for Reliability:** Architect services with resiliency, redundancy, and security in mind.
4. **Monitoring and Measurement:** Track metrics aligned with both utility and warranty to ensure you're meeting the standards you've set.
5. **Continuous Improvement:** Regularly assess service performance and seek ways to enhance both the service's functionality (utility) and its reliability (warranty).

ITIL 4 and Utility and Warranty

ITIL 4 promotes utility and warranty through:

- **Practices:** ITIL practices such as Service Level Management, Capacity and Availability Management, and Information Security Management all support different aspects of warranty.
- **Value Co-creation:** Emphasizes collaboration with customers to define utility and warranty that address their true needs.
- **The Service Value System (SVS):** The SVS ensures all components of the organization work in harmony to deliver both utility and warranty.

The Importance of Balance

Focus too heavily on utility, and you risk a service that overpromises. Focus solely on warranty, and you might create a technically robust service that misses the mark for what users *actually* need.

Additional Resources

- **ITIL 4 Service Level Management (SLM):**
  https://itsm.tools/itil-4-service-level-management/
- **The Difference Between Utility and Warranty:**
  https://www.bmc.com/blogs/itil-4-utility-vs-warranty/

This concludes our section on the fundamentals of Service Management. Are you ready to dive into the core components of the ITIL 4 framework?

Section 3:
Mastering ITIL 4 Essentials

Navigating the Four Dimensions of Service Management

The Four Dimensions of Service Management is a holistic model designed to ensure that all aspects of a service are considered and integrated. These dimensions are essential for creating services that are both valuable and fit for purpose.

Introducing the Four Dimensions

The Four Dimensions of Service Management are:

1. **Organizations and People:** The human element, the structure of the organization(s) involved, and the culture that shapes how services are managed and delivered.
2. **Information and Technology:** The data, knowledge, tools, systems, and technologies that facilitate the provision and management of the service.
3. **Partners and Suppliers:** The network of external organizations that contribute to the value chain, enabling service delivery.
4. **Value Streams and Processes:** The workflows, activities, and controls that transform inputs into outputs, ultimately creating value for the customer.

Why the Four Dimensions Matter

Considering all four dimensions is crucial because:

- **Holistic Perspective:** Prevents focusing too narrowly on one area (like technology) while neglecting others crucial to overall service success
- **Interconnectedness:** Each dimension influences the others. Changes in one area will likely have ripple effects across other dimensions.
- **Balance:** Ensures the right attention and resources are allocated to optimize all aspects of a service.
- **Eliminates Silos:** Encourages collaboration and breaking down barriers between different units and teams.

Navigating Each Dimension

Let's take a brief tour of each dimension:

- **Organizations and People**
  - Organizational structures and roles
  - Skills and competencies
  - Leadership and culture
  - Communication and collaboration
- **Information and Technology**
  - Knowledge and data management
  - Technology architecture and infrastructure
  - Automation capabilities
  - Tools for service management
- **Partners and Suppliers**
  - Supplier selection and relationship management
  - Contracts and agreements
  - Integration of services and capabilities
  - Risk and performance management
- **Value Streams and Processes**
  - Process design and optimization
  - Workflow management tools
  - Governance and decision-making frameworks

- ○ Metrics and measurement for process performance

How ITIL 4 Practices Align

ITIL 4 Practices map to the various aspects of the Four Dimensions:

- **General Management Practices:** Focused on strategy, portfolio management, and organizational aspects.
- **Service Management Practices:** Cover processes like incident management, change enablement, and service design, directly touching value streams and processes.
- **Technical Management Practices:** Address infrastructure, software development, and other technology-focused areas.

Practical Tips

- **Identify Dependencies:** Map out how specific activities within each dimension connect.
- **Visualize Your Ecosystem:** Create diagrams to depict stakeholders, suppliers, and the interactions between different elements of your service ecosystem.
- **Regular Reviews:** Conduct assessments to identify potential imbalances or weaknesses across the dimensions.

Beyond the Basics

The Four Dimensions are always at play. Consciously consider them when:

- **Designing New Services:** Ensure all relevant aspects are incorporated from the outset.
- **Analyzing Problems:** Root cause analysis often uncovers issues in one or more dimensions.
- **Driving Improvements:** Optimize a service holistically rather than focusing on isolated parts.

Additional Resources

- **The Four Dimensions of Service Management – Official AXELOS Overview:**
  https://www.axelos.com/glossary/term/four-dimensions-of-service-management
- **Blog: Understanding the Four Dimensions Model:**
  https://itsm.tools/four-dimensions-model-itil-4/

Ready to delve even deeper into the complexities of these dimensions? Let's do it!

Exploring the Four Dimensions of Service Management

In the previous chapter, we introduced the Four Dimensions of Service Management. Now, let's dissect each dimension, revealing its nuances and how to make the most of this framework.

1. Organizations and People

This dimension encompasses the heart and soul of any service organization. Key areas to consider:

- **Structure and Roles:** How is the service organization designed? Are roles clearly defined with appropriate authority and accountability?
- **Culture:** What mindsets, behaviors, and values guide how people work? Does the culture promote collaboration, innovation, and customer focus?
- **Skills and Competencies:** Do employees possess the necessary knowledge, technical abilities, and soft skills to deliver the service effectively?
- **Communication and Collaboration:** Are there clear communication channels and practices across different teams and functions?
- **Leadership:** Do leaders set a clear vision, empower teams, and foster a culture aligned with service excellence?

Key Challenges and Best Practices:

- **Silos:** Break down organizational silos with cross-functional teams and encourage communication beyond departments.
- **Resistance to Change:** Address change resistance with transparency, open communication, and training.
- **Talent Development:** Invest in continuous learning, upskilling, and knowledge sharing programs.

2. Information and Technology

The backbone of modern services, this dimension focuses on:

- **Information and Knowledge:** How is information captured, organized, shared, and leveraged across the organization?
- **Technologies:** What tools, platforms, and infrastructure support service delivery and management? Think of both customer-facing systems and back-end infrastructure.
- **Automation:** Where can automation streamline processes, reduce errors, and free up employees to focus on higher-value activities?
- **Security and Data Governance:** What measures safeguard information assets and ensure compliance with data regulations?

Key Challenges and Best Practices:

- **Data Integration:** Break down data silos across systems and ensure data flows seamlessly throughout the value chain.
- **Shadow IT:** Maintain visibility and governance over unmanaged technology solutions that might introduce risks.
- **Emerging Technologies:** Proactively assess the potential of new technologies like Artificial Intelligence (AI) or cloud computing.

3. Partners and Suppliers

This dimension recognizes that no organization operates in isolation. Consider:

- **Supplier Ecosystem:** Who are the key suppliers providing essential resources, goods, or services that contribute to your service?
- **Relationship Management:** How do you build and maintain strong, collaborative relationships with suppliers?

- **Performance and Risk Management:** How do you monitor supplier performance, address risks they introduce, and ensure compliance with requirements?
- **Contract Management:** Are contracts (including SLAs) clear, comprehensive, and designed to manage the relationship effectively?

Key Challenges and Best Practices

- **Dependency Risks:** Proactively manage risks associated with reliance on external suppliers.
- **Communication and Alignment:** Foster open communication channels and align goals with suppliers for mutual benefit.
- **Strategic Partnerships:** Move beyond transactional relationships to strategic partnerships focused on innovation and value co-creation.

4. Value Streams and Processes

Here, the focus lies on how services are designed and delivered. Think about:

- **Value Stream Mapping:** Visually analyze the sequence of steps required to create value for customers, identifying bottlenecks and improvement opportunities.
- **Process Design:** Create processes that are efficient, effective, and aligned with customer needs.
- **Workflow Automation:** Leverage automation to optimize processes where possible.
- **Governance and Controls:** Establish clear decision-making frameworks, control mechanisms, and metrics to monitor process effectiveness.

Key Challenges and Best Practices:

- **Process Complexity:** Aim for simplicity and clarity in process design to boost efficiency and reduce confusion.
- **Lack of Visibility:** Track relevant metrics to gain insights into process performance and pinpoint improvement areas.
- **Continuous Improvement:** Embrace a culture of constant process refinement, empowering your teams to seek out and implement enhancements.

The Interconnectedness of the Dimensions

Remember, changes in one dimension ripple throughout the service ecosystem. For instance, introducing a new technology tool (Information & Technology) will likely have impacts on processes (Value Streams & Processes), people (roles and training needs), and even relationships with suppliers.

Additional Resources

- **AXELOS Resources on the Four Dimensions:** https://www.axelos.com/search?search=Four%20Dimensions
- **Blog: Understanding ITIL 4's Four Dimensions (with Examples):** https://blog.sysaid.com/itil-4-four-dimensions/

Next, let's explore the central nervous system of ITIL 4 – the Service Value System!

Unravelling the Service Value System

Think of the Service Value System as the engine that powers service delivery. It's not a rigidly defined process, but a flexible system designed to support organizations in creating value with their services. Let's break down its key elements:

The SVS Diagram

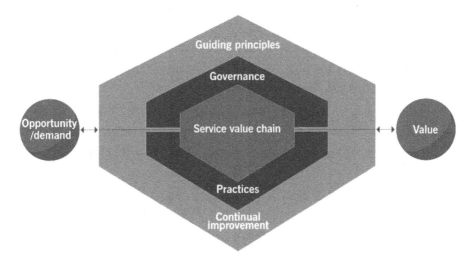

The SVS is often represented as a diagram that includes:

- **Guiding Principles:** Universal recommendations that guide decision-making throughout the service organization.
- **Governance:** Mechanisms that set direction, evaluate performance, and ensure alignment of activities with the organization's goals.
- **Service Value Chain:** The set of key activities that transform inputs into valuable outputs.
- **Practices:** Resources (competencies, processes, tools) designed to perform work efficiently and effectively.

- **Continual Improvement:** The ongoing pursuit of enhancing services and practices at all levels.
- **The Central Core:** Representing the inputs:
    - Opportunity/Demand: The impetus for a new service or change to an existing one.
    - Value: The ultimate goal of all service activities – the co-created benefits for both customer and service provider.

Key Components of the SVS

Let's explore each component in more detail:

1. **Guiding Principles:** We'll cover these in depth in the next chapter, but they provide a philosophical foundation for successful service management.
2. **Governance:** Ensures the organization has clear oversight, decision-making frameworks, evaluation mechanisms, and alignment of service activities with broader strategic objectives.
3. **Service Value Chain:** The core operational model of ITIL 4, comprised of interconnected activities that create value through services. We'll delve into these activities later.
4. **Practices:** Bundled sets of resources designed to achieve specific objectives. ITIL 4 outlines 34 distinct management practices.
5. **Continual Improvement:** A cornerstone philosophy, embedded across the SVS to encourage the continuous enhancement of every aspect of service provision.

Interplay within the SVS

The magic of the SVS lies in the dynamic interaction between its components:

- **Demand triggers value chain activities:** A service request or opportunity initiates actions within the value chain.

- **Practices support value chain activities:** Relevant practices provide the tools, procedures, and resources needed.
- **Guiding principles inform choices:** Decision-making throughout the value chain is guided by the ITIL principles.
- **Governance oversees the system:** Governance mechanisms ensure alignment, accountability, and compliance.
- **Continual improvement drives optimization:** Feedback loops and improvement initiatives work to constantly enhance all parts of the system.

The SVS in Practice

The SVS is not prescriptive; here's how it is utilized:

- **Adapt to Your Organization:** Tailor the SVS to your unique needs and structure. Not all practices will be equally relevant; focus on what brings value in your context.
- **Visualize Your SVS:** Create a diagram that reflects your specific practices and how they fit within your value chains. This enhances communication and collaboration.
- **Start Where it Matters:** Don't try to perfect everything at once. Use the SVS to diagnose pain points and prioritize areas for improvement.

Beyond the Diagram

The SVS is about more than its visual representation. Consider:

- **Culture and Mindset:** The SVS thrives in a culture of value co-creation, customer-centricity, and continual improvement.
- **External Factors:** Be mindful of trends in the market, technology, and regulations that shape the demand and how you deliver your services. The SVS is a dynamic system!

Additional Resources

- **AXELOS Overview of the Service Value System:**
  https://www.axelos.com/svs-overview
- **SVS Explained: Visual Blog Post:**
  https://www.example.com/svs-explained-visual-blog-post

Now, let's turn our attention to one of the most powerful components of the SVS, the ITIL Guiding Principles!

Embracing Guiding Principles for Success

ITIL 4's Guiding Principles are a set of universal recommendations that help organizations adopt and adapt ITIL in different situations. They promote a mindset conducive to effective service management, regardless of specific technologies, methodologies, or organizational structures you use.

The Seven Guiding Principles

Let's explore each of the seven principles in ITIL 4:

1. **Focus on Value:** Every decision, action, and service should align with the ultimate purpose: creating value for customers and stakeholders.
2. **Start Where You Are:** Don't discard what works. Build upon existing processes, successes, and resources rather than starting from scratch.
3. **Progress Iteratively with Feedback:** Take incremental steps, incorporate feedback loops and continuously learn and refine your services over time.
4. **Collaborate and Promote Visibility:** Break down silos! Foster transparency, open communication, and teamwork throughout the service ecosystem.
5. **Think and Work Holistically:** Never lose sight of the big picture. Consider the impact of changes on the wider service and all dimensions (Organizations & People, Value Streams & Processes, etc.).
6. **Keep it Simple and Practical:** Avoid complexity and bureaucracy. Streamline practices and aim for solutions that are pragmatic and easy to implement.
7. **Optimize and Automate:** Leverage technology to improve efficiency and free up resources to focus on innovation.

Remember, automate with care, ensuring it enhances rather than hinders the human touch.

Why the Guiding Principles Matter

The Guiding Principles offer several benefits:

- **Universal Guidance:** They are applicable in any service management context, regardless of your industry or technology stacks.
- **Adaptability:** They encourage flexible, context-driven solutions rather than rigid rules.
- **Sound Decision-Making:** They provide a framework for evaluating options and making choices aligned with successful service management.
- **Resilience:** They help adapt effectively to changing circumstances, market shifts, or unexpected events.

Putting the Principles into Practice

Tips for applying them effectively:

- **Make Them Visible:** Communicate the guiding principles across your organization, making them part of everyday conversations and decision-making.
- **Use them in Scenarios:** Challenge teams with real-world scenarios and use the principles to analyze issues and brainstorm solutions.
- **Embed in Training:** Integrate the principles into all levels of service management training and onboarding.
- **Celebrate Success Stories:** Acknowledge and reward individuals who exemplify the guiding principles in their work.

Examples of Principles in Action

Let's see how the principles translate into action:

- **Focus on Value:** Regularly assess if services are still achieving their intended outcomes for customers.
- **Progress Iteratively with Feedback:** Launch a service as a Minimum Viable Product (MVP), gather user feedback, and swiftly iterate on its design.
- **Think and Work Holistically:** Before launching a new self-service portal (Info & Tech), assess impacts on the workload of the support team (Org & People) and potential updates needed to knowledge management (Info & Tech).

The Power of Combining Principles

Often, the greatest insights come from applying multiple principles together. For example:

- **"Focus on Value" + "Think and Work Holistically"** Reminds you to consider the value for all stakeholders, not just the end customer.
- **"Progress Iteratively with Feedback" + "Optimize and Automate"** Encourages using automation to streamline feedback mechanisms and accelerate improvements.

Additional Resources

- **AXELOS Overview of the ITIL Guiding Principles:** https://www.axelos.com/best-practice-solutions/itil/itil-guiding-principles
- **Blog: How to Apply the Guiding Principles of ITIL for Organizational Success:** https://www.exampleblog.com/apply-guiding-principles-itil-organizational-success

Embarking on the Service Value Chain Journey

The Service Value Chain is the core operational model within the ITIL 4 Service Value System. It depicts a set of interconnected activities that service organizations perform to co-create value through services.

Dissecting the Service Value Chain

While the SVC is often visualized as a linear process, it's important to understand it's a highly flexible model that can adapt and flow depending on specific needs and scenarios. The key activities include:

1. **Plan:** Defines the strategic direction, establishes portfolios of services, and sets out the architecture for service provision.
2. **Improve:** A continuous activity that ensures all aspects of the service and the organization are constantly enhancing how they create value.
3. **Engage:** Builds positive relationships with stakeholders, understands user needs, fosters transparency, and ensures a great user experience.
4. **Design & Transition:** Designs new services or modifications to existing ones, ensuring they align with user needs, meet requirements, and seamlessly transition into live environments.
5. **Obtain/Build:** Acquires or builds required service components, whether it's technology, teams, partnerships, or service components.
6. **Deliver & Support:** Ensures that services are delivered and supported as per agreed-upon terms, meeting the

needs of users and providing them with a positive experience.

Demand and Value

The entire Service Value Chain is bookended by two crucial elements:

- **Demand:** Can be a new opportunity, a need for change, or a request for a service. It triggers activity within the SVC.
- **Value:** The desired outcomes co-created by the service provider and the service consumer, representing the ultimate goal of the SVC activities.

Key Concepts of the SVC

- **Flexible, not rigid:** The SVC isn't a prescriptive step-by-step process. Adapt and configure it to best suit your specific requirements and scenarios.
- **Value Streams:** Within the SVC, specific sequences of activities create specific value streams. Organizations might have multiple value streams for different service scenarios.
- **Iterative:** Activities in the SVC aren't always sequential, often there are feedback loops and iterations between various activities.

How ITIL 4 Practices Fit In

ITIL 4's 34 management practices directly support the different activities of the SVC:

- **Planning Practices:** General management practices like Portfolio Management or Strategy Management
- **Improvement Practices:** Continual Improvement or Measurement and Reporting
- **Engagement Practices:** Business Relationship Management or Service Level Management

- …And many others tailored to specific aspects of the SVC!

Starting Your SVC Journey

Here's how to make this practical:

1. **Understand the "As-Is":** Map your current processes and activities. It's okay if it doesn't perfectly align with the ITIL 4 SVC – that's your starting point.
2. **Identify Value Streams:** Analyze how you co-create value currently. What are the specific sequences of steps for different service scenarios?
3. **Prioritize Improvements:** Aligned with your strategic goals, identify pain points or areas where improvements will yield the highest "return on value".
4. **Leverage ITIL Practices:** Select appropriate ITIL 4 practices to help optimize your activities in targeted areas.

Visualizing the SVC

Representing your SVC as a diagram offers several advantages:

- **Common Understanding:** Provides a shared view of how value flows within your organization.
- **Identifies Bottlenecks:** Helps visualize areas where processes or activities are slow or inefficient.
- **Collaboration:** Fosters communication between different teams and highlights areas of interdependence.

Additional Resources

- **AXELOS Overview of the Service Value Chain:** https://www.axelos.com/best-practice-solutions/itil/what-is-itil/itil-4-the-service-value-chain
- **Mapping Value Streams in ITIL 4 (Blog):** https://www.everbridge.com/blog/mapping-value-streams-in-itil-4/

Ready to delve into how to move up the levels of service management maturity as you optimize your Service Value Chain? Let's talk about advancing through the SVC activities.

Advancing through the Service Value Chain

The Service Value Chain isn't a static model; it's designed to evolve and mature as your organization grows. As you master the core SVC activities, your focus shifts to how you can refine these activities, create more seamless value flows, and ultimately boost value co-creation.

Continuous Improvement Mindset

Continual improvement, a core element of the Service Value System, is the engine of SVC advancement. Adopt continuous improvement as a philosophy in the following key areas:

- **Optimize Processes:** Analyze each activity of the SVC, seek out ways to streamline workflows, eliminate redundancy, and maximize efficiency.
- **Leverage Automation:** Identify opportunities to automate repetitive, manual tasks within SVC activities, freeing up employees for higher-value work and reducing errors.
- **Data-Driven Decisions:** Track metrics related to SVC performance and use insights to identify bottlenecks, areas for optimization, and prioritize improvements.

Levels of SVC Activity Maturity

Maturity levels help conceptualize how you can gradually refine your Service Value Chain:

- **Basic:** Initial implementation of SVC activities. Processes are likely ad hoc and reactive, with a focus on functionality.
- **Intermediate:** SVC activities are more consistent and defined. There's a focus on effectiveness and meeting agreed-upon service levels.

- **Advanced:** SVC activities are proactive and highly optimized. There's a focus on agility, innovation, and exceeding customer expectations.

Moving Up the Maturity Ladder

Here's how to ascend the SVC maturity curve:

1. **Assess Current State:** Honestly evaluate where you are with each SVC activity. Consider efficiency, stability, and user satisfaction for each.
2. **Set Target State:** Define your desired maturity level for each activity, aligning it with your strategic goals as a service provider.
3. **Prioritize Improvements:** Don't try to fix everything at once. Focus on improvements within the SVC that will yield the best return in terms of value creation.
4. **Embrace Tooling and Technology:** Investigate tools and technologies that can support SVC improvements:
   - Workflow automation tools
   - Service management platforms
   - Advanced analytics capabilities

Key Success Factors for Advancing

Let's look at enablers of continual SVC improvement:

- **Leadership Support:** Maturity requires investment and commitment. Leaders must set the tone and allocate resources accordingly.
- **Culture of Improvement:** Encourage a culture where seeking out improvement opportunities and experimenting with new approaches is celebrated.
- **Knowledge Sharing:** Facilitate collaboration and knowledge transfer so teams can learn from each other and avoid siloed improvements.

- **Partner Collaboration:** If your value chain relies on partners and suppliers, work together with them on continuous improvement efforts.

Focus on Specific SVC Activities

Examples of how to enhance specific SVC activities:

- **Plan:** Introduce robust demand forecasting methods to better manage capacity and resources.
- **Engage:** Adopt a proactive approach to identifying potential issues and resolving them before they negatively impact the customer's experience.
- **Design & Transition:** Implement DevOps methodologies to smooth the flow from development into live environments, increasing change success rates.
- **Deliver & Support:** Move from reactive incident management to proactive problem management, addressing potential issues before they cause widespread outages.

Additional Resources

- **Blog: ITIL 4 Maturity Models for Service Management Improvement**
  https://blog.sysaid.com/itil-4-maturity-models-for-service-management-improvement/
- **Using Value Stream Mapping for Continual Improvement:**
  https://www.lean.org/WhatsLean/Principles.cfm

The Role of Continual Improvement

Now that we've discussed the Service Value Chain and its continuous optimization, let's solidify your understanding by exploring the cornerstone ITIL 4 practice of Continual Improvement.

Embracing Continual Improvement

In the dynamic world of services, standing still is equivalent to moving backward. Continual Improvement is a foundational philosophy within ITIL 4, encouraging relentless pursuit of service enhancements. This practice empowers organizations to adapt, innovate, and unlock ever-greater levels of value.

What is Continual Improvement in ITIL 4?

ITIL 4 defines Continual Improvement as: **"A recurring organizational activity performed at all levels to ensure that an organization's performance continually meets stakeholders' expectations."**

Key Concepts:

- **Embedded Everywhere:** The mindset of Continual Improvement should permeate all aspects of the service organization and across all levels.
- **Iterative:** Improvement is achieved through small, incremental steps rather than big-bang disruptive changes.
- **Everyone's Responsibility:** While there might be dedicated roles for improvement, everyone has a part to play in identifying and acting on improvement opportunities.

Why Continual Improvement Matters

In the realm of service management, Continual Improvement is essential due to:

- **Evolving Customer Needs:** Ensures services keep pace with changing expectations and remain relevant.

- **Technological Advancements:** Allows organizations to adapt and harness new technologies to enhance their offerings.
- **Competitive Pressure:** Helps maintain a competitive edge in the market by continually improving efficiency and value proposition.
- **Resilience:** The ability to constantly learn and improve is crucial for surviving and thriving in the face of disruptions.

The Continual Improvement Model (CIM)

ITIL 4 provides a structured approach for driving improvement:

1. **What is the vision?** Define the desired future state, goals, or objectives of your improvement efforts.
2. **Where are we now?** Establish a baseline of performance by assessing the current state of your service, process, or organization.
3. **Where do we want to be?** Set specific, measurable, and time-bound improvement targets aligned with your vision.
4. **How do we get there?** Design and implement improvement initiatives. This could involve process optimization, adopting new technologies, or skills development.
5. **Take action!** Execute the initiatives, track progress, and refine as needed.
6. **Did we get there?** Evaluate the outcomes of your improvements against your targets. Capture and share lessons learned.
7. **How do we keep the momentum going?** Continual Improvement is never finished! Ensure improvements are sustainable and identify the next areas for betterment.

Tools and Techniques for Continual Improvement

- **PDCA (Plan-Do-Check-Act):** A classic cyclical model for structured improvement.
- **Value Stream Mapping:** Visualize your process flows to identify bottlenecks and inefficiencies.
- **Root Cause Analysis (RCA):** Dig deep to uncover the underlying cause of problems, preventing recurrence.
- **Lean and Six Sigma:** Methodologies with a variety of tools and concepts for efficiency and waste reduction.

Cultivating a Culture of Improvement

The true impact of Continual Improvement comes from mindset:

- **Growth Mindset:** Encourage a culture of learning, embracing failures as opportunities.
- **Celebrate Wins:** Acknowledge and reward improvement efforts, both big and small.
- **Psychological Safety:** Build an environment where team members feel safe to suggest ideas and identify issues without fear of reprisal.
- **Data-Driven Approach:** Use metrics and feedback loops to make improvement efforts transparent and measurable.

Additional Resources:

- **ITIL 4 Continual Improvement Practice Overview:** https://www.axelos.com/search?q=ITIL+4+Continual+Improvement+Practice+Overview
- **Techniques for Continual Improvement:** https://www.bmc.com/blogs/itil-techniques-continual-service-improvement/

Delving into the Essential Practices: A Deep Dive

ITIL 4's Management Practices provide structured toolkits for performing work across the service organization. They bundle together resources, processes, and capabilities to address specific service management challenges.

Types of Practices

ITIL 4 organizes the 34 practices into three categories:

1. **General Management Practices (14):** Practices applicable across various areas of service management and beyond IT. Examples include:
   - Strategy Management
   - Portfolio Management
   - Risk Management
   - Financial Management
2. **Service Management Practices (17):** Practices specifically designed to support different aspects of service delivery. Examples include:
   - Incident Management
   - Change Enablement
   - Service Level Management
   - Service Design
3. **Technical Management Practices (3):** Focus on the management of technology within the context of services. Examples include:
   - Deployment Management
   - Infrastructure and Platform Management
   - Software Development and Management

Understanding Each Practice

Key components to understand within each practice are:

- **Purpose:** The reason the practice exists and the specific challenges it addresses.
- **Scope:** What the practice covers and any boundaries or limitations.
- **Key Concepts:** Fundamental concepts, terminology, or models that form the basis of the practice.
- **Processes and Activities:** The workflow steps and actions involved.
- **Roles and Responsibilities:** Who carries out the activities and who holds decision-making authority.
- **Tools and Technologies:** Supporting technologies that streamline and automate tasks within the practice.

Important Note: Practices are Adaptable

ITIL 4 practices aren't rigid. Consider these points:

- **Tailor them:** Adapt practices to suit the specific needs and scale of your organization. Focus on adding value, not strictly adhering to every prescriptive detail.
- **Don't implement them all at once:** Prioritize the practices that address your most pressing concerns or yield the greatest benefit.
- **Continuous Improvement:** Regularly review the effectiveness of your practices and adapt them as needed.

How to Choose the Right Practices

Selecting practices to delve into depends on:

- **Challenges you face:** If struggling with incident management, deep dive into Incident Management.
- **Strategic goals:** Prioritize practices like Project Management or Portfolio Management for alignment with high-level objectives.

- **Industry and Context:** Research industry-specific recommendations. Practices relevant to healthcare differ from those in software development.
- **Maturity:** Don't overcomplicate things early on. Master basic practices before moving to more advanced ones.

Where to Learn More

- **AXELOS Overview of all ITIL 4 Practices:** https://www.axelos.com/best-practice-solutions/itil/itil-4-framework

A Word of Caution

Remember, practices are a means to an end, not the end itself. Avoid excessive focus on process alone. Always link the practices back to how they ultimately facilitate value creation for your customers and stakeholders.

Additional Resources

- **ITIL® 4 - A Pocket Guide** https://www.amazon.com/ITIL%C2%AE-Pocket-Guide-Van-Haren/dp/9401807979

In our final chapter, let's explore how to pull these concepts together and achieve an integrated approach to service excellence.

Integration: Connecting the Dots

True excellence in service management demands an integrated perspective. While ITIL 4 provides a powerful framework of individual concepts and practices, it's how they interweave and support each other that leads to exceptional results. This chapter focuses on achieving integration.

Why Integration Matters

Here's why a deliberate approach to integration is crucial:

- **Break Down Silos:** Integration encourages dismantling silos between departments, teams, and processes. This is crucial for smooth value flows.
- **Optimize the Whole:** Optimizing isolated parts won't necessarily optimize the entire service. Integration helps ensure changes in one area have positive impacts throughout the service ecosystem.
- **Consistency and User Experience:** Integrated processes and practices lead to a more seamless and consistent experience for service users.
- **Efficiency and Cost-Effectiveness:** Integration helps avoid duplication of efforts, reduces re-work, and improves resource utilization.
- **Agility and Resilience:** A well-integrated service organization can adapt swiftly to changes in demand, new technologies, or unexpected disruptions.

Key Areas to Focus on for Integration

Let's look at where integration efforts are essential:

1. **Integration Across the Four Dimensions:** Ensure that processes, technology decisions, organizational structures, and skills development all work harmoniously, with an understanding of the inter-play between these areas.
2. **Integration within the Service Value Chain:** Each activity in your SVC must connect smoothly to the next. Focus on optimizing transitions and flows between the activities of your value chain.
3. **Integration of Practices:** Avoid applying practices in a vacuum. Consider how they connect. Incident Management findings might drive Problem Management activities, or changes might trigger updates to your Service Catalog.
4. **Integration with Tools and Technologies:** Service management tools shouldn't create islands of information. Ensure data flows between them, enhancing visibility and decision-making. Look for tools designed to work together.
5. **Integration with external partners/suppliers:** Align your processes and expectations to build a cohesive value chain across organizations that contribute to your service.

How to Achieve Integration

Here are practical approaches to fostering better integration:

- **Process Mapping:** Visualize how different processes and activities interconnect across the organization. Look for bottlenecks and hand-off points.
- **Data Integration:** Ensure that data collected in various practices and tools can be shared and analyzed to identify trends and improvement opportunities.
- **Knowledge Management:** Establish a central knowledge base accessible across teams and departments, preventing duplicate effort and enabling effective collaboration.
- **Cross-functional Teams:** Include members from various functions on improvement initiatives, breaking down siloed thinking and building shared understanding.

The Role of Governance

Governance is essential for sustainable integration:

- **Clear Decision-making:** Establish governance mechanisms to guide how integrated decisions are made, resolving conflicting priorities across teams/functions.
- **Architecture:** Develop a cohesive architecture that aligns technology, processes across systems, and service components.
- **Metrics and Monitoring:** Track metrics that reflect end-to-end value delivery, not just isolated process metrics.

Integration in Action: A Common Scenario

Problem: Slow and ineffective resolution of major customer-impacting incidents.

Integrated Approach:

- Examine contributing factors across multiple practices (Incident Management, Problem Management, Change Enablement)
- Analyze data and process flows across the Four Dimensions to pinpoint root cause
- Implement holistic solutions (process improvements, knowledge sharing initiatives, enhanced monitoring automation, or vendor contract revision)

Additional Resources

- **Blog : Why Integration is Key to ITIL 4 Success:** https://itsm.tools/2019/10/09/itil-4-integration-service-management-success/
- **The Critical Role of Governance in Integrating Service Management Systems**

https://www.sciencedirect.com/science/article/pii/S1877050
91401593X

Integration: Synthesizing Concepts for Implementation

Throughout this book, you've gained a robust understanding of the key components of ITIL 4. The true test is how you now synthesize and apply this knowledge to drive tangible improvements in your service management practices. Let's explore strategies for successful implementation.

Start with "Why"

Before anything else, always articulate:

- **Business Goals:** What specific business challenges or opportunities are you addressing through ITIL 4 adoption?
- **Desired Outcomes:** How will ITIL 4 help achieve value for customers and the organization as a whole?

Adopting, Not Just Adapting

ITIL 4 emphasizes purposeful adaptation to meet your unique needs. However, start with these principles during initial implementation:

- **Think Big, Start Small:** Have a holistic vision of long-term service management transformation, but begin with targeted, high-impact initiatives to build momentum.
- **Prioritize Value:** Identify areas where ITIL 4 practices and concepts can quickly address pain points or unlock potential value.
- **Phased Roll-out:** Don't try to implement everything at once. Prioritize practices, introduce them in stages, and iterate based on feedback.

Key Steps for Successful Implementation

1. **Assessment and Baselining:**
   - Analyze the current state of your service management processes and capabilities. Identify gaps, inefficiencies, and pain points.
2. **Strategic Roadmap:**
   - Develop a high-level plan aligning with business goals, and establish a timeline for implementation that includes smaller milestones along the way.
3. **Prioritization:**
   - Choose specific ITIL 4 practices that will address the most compelling gaps or deliver valuable impact in the fastest way.
   - Consider using a 'maturity model' to assess your current state and set goals for improvement.
4. **Communication and Education:**
   - Proactively address the "what's in it for me?" question across stakeholders at all levels, tailoring messages for different audiences (executives to team members).
   - Invest in training to build understanding of ITIL concepts and how they will be applied within the organization.
5. **Technology and Tooling**:
   - Assess existing tools and determine if they support chosen ITIL 4 practices, or plan technology upgrades/replacements where necessary.
6. **Pilot Projects:**
   - Start with pilot implementations in a controlled environment, collect feedback, refine the approach, then scale-up successful practices.
7. **Metrics and Measurement:**
   - Define KPIs that align with the goals you set initially. Track your progress against these metrics to measure impact and identify further improvement opportunities.

- o Don't focus solely on process metrics; align KPIs with value-driven outcomes.

Keys to Overcome Challenges

Let's be realistic, implementation isn't always smooth. Here's how to address common hurdles:

- **Resistance to Change:**
  - o Address the fears of impacted staff. Transparent communication, training, and success stories help ease resistance.
- **Lack of Resources:**
  - o Demonstrate a clear return on investment for ITIL-driven initiatives to secure buy-in and support from leadership.
- **Cultural Mindset:**
  - o Cultivate a customer-centric, collaborative, and improvement-oriented culture. Emphasize the guiding principles, ensuring they are embedded in everyday behaviors.

Visualization as a Tool

Illustrative diagrams can simplify complexity, and enhance communication:

- **Conceptual Model Visualization:** Diagram how elements of ITIL 4 (SVS, Four Dimensions, select practices) interact within your organization.
- **Process Maps:** Map your current and future-state (with ITIL) processes to aid implementation.

Continuous Learning and Adaptation

- **Embrace Feedback:** Gather insights from stakeholders, be open to criticism, and incorporate feedback for continuous evolution.
- **Community Engagement:** Tap into ITIL communities to learn from others – share your successes and failures, aiding the wider industry.

Conclusion

Remember, ITIL 4 is a journey, not a destination. Consistent improvement and adaptation in response to an ever-evolving landscape is the true mark of a service management leader. Let the concepts and practices offered in this book be tools to empower your organization on the road toward service excellence.

Additional Resources

- **ITIL® Success Stories and Case Studies**
  https://www.axelos.com/case-studies?product=itil
- **ITIL® Practitioner Certification Level**
  https://www.axelos.com/certifications/itil-certifications/itil-practitioner-certification (For those seeking to learn more about practical implementation)

I hope you found this guide valuable. Best of luck in your service management endeavors!

Conclusion

As you reach the end of this guide, you've been equipped with a deep understanding of ITIL 4, its key concepts, and a blueprint for applying this knowledge. Remember, ITIL 4 isn't just a set of rules, but a mindset that prioritizes value creation, pragmatism, and a holistic approach to service management.

Key Takeaways

Let's recap some of the most powerful lessons from our exploration:

- **The Value Imperative:** Always focus on how your services create value for customers, stakeholders, and the organization itself. Let value be your guiding star.
- **Four Dimensions in Harmony:** Consider the interplay between people, technology, processes, and partnerships. Decisions must consider impacts across all dimensions for optimal outcomes.
- **The Power of the SVS:** The Service Value System provides a dynamic framework to guide how you turn potential value into reality, and a common language within your organization.
- **Guiding Principles as Your Compass:** In moments of doubt, turn to the ITIL guiding principles for sound decision-making, ensuring you remain aligned with the fundamentals of good service management.
- **The Service Value Chain: Activity Hub** Understand how this core model drives value creation and seek to optimize and enhance each activity within your SVC.
- **Continual Improvement as a Way of Life:** Embrace change and view every moment, success or setback, as an opportunity to improve and refine the services you provide.

- **Success Through Integration:** Strive to break down silos and build a service ecosystem where processes, technologies, teams, and knowledge flow seamlessly in the pursuit of shared goals.

From Knowledge to Action

ITIL 4 only reaches its potential when put into practice. Consider these action points:

- **Start Your Assessment:** Begin by evaluating your organization's current service management practices through the lens of ITIL 4.
- **Identify Quick Wins:** Select areas where targeted ITIL practices or principles can deliver high-impact improvements early on to build momentum and buy-in.
- **Experiment and Learn:** Don't be afraid to pilot new approaches or tailor practices. Adopt an iterative mindset, celebrating both successes and failures as learning opportunities.

Continuous Evolution

Service management excellence is not a destination, but an ongoing pursuit. Stay engaged with the broader ITIL community, seek continuous learning opportunities, and adapt in response to the evolving needs of your customers and changing technologies.

Your journey starts now. Let the lessons from this book equip you to become a leader in service management, driving value creation, customer satisfaction, and the overall success of your organization.

I wish you the very best in your service management endeavors!

www.ingramcontent.com/pod-product-compliance
Lightning Source LLC
LaVergne TN
LVHW081531050326
832903LV00025B/1731